Sick of Each Other

WILLIAM STEIG

JOANNA COTLER BOOKS
An Imprint of HarperCollins*Publishers*

Sick of Each Other

Copyright © 2001 by William Steig

Printed in the U.S.A. All rights reserved.

www.harperchildrens.com

Library of Congress Cataloging-in-Publication Data is available.

ISBN 0-06-029555-4

Typography by Alicia Mikles

1 2 3 4 5 6 7 8 9 10

❖

First Edition

Okay, Jeanne?

I've a feeling this is not going to work.

I thought we were having fun.

Shove it.

He's such a dog!

But you are a part of me!

What a drag!

The thrill is gone.

This cocktail will kill him.

We're just not in tune.

I bet <u>he's</u> not married.

Are we at an impasse?

You <u>make</u> me yell at you!

I also hate your tears.

Well, I <u>feel</u> like the devil!

Dissatisfied? Why would I be dissatisfied?

And Polly agrees with me!

Who asked you to rescue me?

I'm the one who's being reasonable!

I'm tired of this sticky relationship.

They'd believe me . . . people drown all the time.

Say you adore me.